PROFITABLE FLOWER GARDENING FOR BEGINNERS

FLOWER GARDENER'S GUIDE TO GROWING FLOWERS FOR PROFIT

ROSE MEYER

COPYRIGHT

DEDICATION

This book is dedicated to all of the amazing people who have supported me, no matter what. Thank you for your love and understanding. Thank you for taking out time and money to get this Book -- you're always here in my heart!

TABLE OF CONTENTS

ABOUT THE BOOK

Flower gardening is a rewarding and therapeutic hobby that anyone can enjoy. With a little know-how, it can be quite profitable too! If you're thinking of starting a flower garden, then "Profitable Flower Gardening for Beginners" is the perfect book for you.

This comprehensive guide covers everything you need to know to get started, from choosing the right flowers and plants to soil preparation, planting, and maintenance. You'll also learn about the different ways to market your flowers, whether you plan to sell them at farmers markets or through a floral delivery service. With clear instructions and plenty of practical tips, "Profitable Flower Gardening for Beginners" is essential reading for anyone interested in this fulfilling pursuit.

INTRODUCTION

Flower farming is a centuries-old tradition that has been passed down from generation to generation. The origins of flower farming can be traced back to the middle Ages when European monks began growing flowers in monastery gardens. In the years that followed, the popularity of flower farming spread to other parts of Europe, and by the 1800s, it had become a thriving industry in countries like France and Holland. In recent years, the popularity of flower farming has grown exponentially, with farms popping up all over the world. Today, flower farmers are able to utilize cutting-edge technologies to produce beautiful blooms that are enjoyed by people all over the globe.

Growing a flower farm can be a challenging and rewarding experience. To get started, you'll need to choose a location that gets plenty of sunlight and has well-draining soil. Once you've selected a spot, you'll need to clear any debris and level the ground. Next, you'll need to build raised beds or dig trenches for your plants. Flower farming is a labor-intensive venture, so you'll need to be prepared to put in long hours during the planting and harvesting season. However, the rewards of working with nature to create beautiful blooms are more than worth the effort. With careful planning and hard work, you can turn your flower farm into a thriving business.

CHAPTER 1
FLOWER FARM GUIDE

If you're thinking of starting a flower farm, there are a few things you'll need to take into account. First of all, you'll need to choose the right location. Make sure you have plenty of space for both growing and storing your flowers, and that the climate is conducive to flower growth. You'll also need to decide what type of flowers you want to grow. Will you specialize in a particular type of flower, or grow a variety of flowers? Once you've got the basics sorted out, it's time to get down to business.

Here are a few tips on how to grow a successful flower farm:

1. Start small: It's important not to bite off more than you can chew when you're first starting out. Don't try to grow too many different types of flowers, or expand your operation too quickly. Start with a manageable number of plants, and gradually increase your inventory as you get more experience.

2. Be strategic about your plantings: One key to success is ensuring that your plants are properly spaced and positioned for optimal growth. This includes taking into account things like sunlight exposure, drainage, and soil type.

3. Keep an eye on the forecast: Make sure you know when rainfall is expected, so you can provide adequate water for your plants (without overwatering them). Likewise, be aware of potential frost dates in your area, and take steps to protect your plants if necessary. By covering them or bringing them indoors temporarily.)

4. Harvest at the right time: Timing is everything when it comes to harvesting your flowers. Cut them too early, and they won't be at their peak; cut them too late, and they'll be past their prime. Pay close attention to your plants, and harvest when they're looking their best.

5. Have a plan for marketing and selling your flowers once they're harvested: Whether you sell them directly to customers at farmer's markets or through a local florist, it's important to have a plan in place so you can get your flowers into the hands of those who will appreciate them most!

Flower garden

A flower garden is a great way to add color and beauty to your yard. But before you start planting, there are a few things you need to know. First, decide what kind of flowers you want to grow. Annuals and perennials are the most popular choices, but there are also many options for native plants and wildflowers. Once you've selected your flowers, you'll need to choose the right location for your garden. Make sure to choose a spot that gets plenty of sunlight and has well-drained soil. You'll also want to consider the size of your garden. If you're limited on space, you can always opt for potted plants instead. Once you have all of these details figured out, it's time to start planting!

Flower garden for beginners

For anyone who has ever dreamed of starting their own flower garden, the prospect can seem daunting. Where do you start? What kind of flowers should you choose? How do you keep them healthy and happy? Never fear, fellow gardening novice! With a little planning and elbow grease, you can create a blooming oasis in no time.

One of the first things to consider when starting a flower garden is your climate. Certain flowers will only thrive in specific conditions, so it's important to pick varieties that will do well in your neck of the woods. Once you've got that sorted, it's time to roll up your sleeves and get to work preparing the soil. This step is key to ensuring that your flowers have the nutrients they need to grow strong and healthy. After all, even the most beautiful blooms can't flourish in poor-quality earth.

Next, it's time to choose your plants! When selecting flowers for your garden, take into account both their appearance and their care requirements. Some varieties require more attention than others, and you don't want your dream garden to turn into a high-maintenance nightmare. Once you've made your purchases, it's time for the fun part: planting! Be sure to give each bloom plenty of space to spread its roots, and water regularly according to each plant's needs. With a little care and patience, you'll soon have a stunning garden that will bring you joy for years to come.

Structuring a flower garden

When planning a flower garden, there are a few things to keep in mind.

- First, consider the size of the garden and the amount of sun or shade it receives. This will help you determine which plants will thrive in the space.

- Second, think about the color scheme you want to create. Do you want a garden that is full of vibrant colors, or something more subdued? Once you have an idea of what you want, it's time to start planning your layout.

- Sketch out a basic design, then fill in the details. Don't be afraid to experiment - part of the fun of gardening is seeing how your plants grow and change over time. With a little planning, you can create a beautiful flower garden that will provide you with enjoyment for years to come.

Best Flowers for a home garden

If you're looking to add some color to your home garden, you might be wondering which flowers are the best to choose. There are a few factors to consider, such as climate and soil type. But with so many beautiful blooms to choose from, it can be hard to decide which ones are right for you. Here are a few of our favorite flowers for home gardens:

- Roses - With their wide range of colors and types, roses are a classic choice for any garden. They prefer full sun and well-drained soil, and they come in both bush and climbing varieties.

- Tulips - One of the first signs of spring, tulips are a popular choice for gardens. They come in a wide range of colors, and they're relatively easy to care for. Tulips prefer full sun and well-drained soil.

- Lilies – The famous Lilies come in many different shapes and sizes, and they're a popular choice for gardens. They come in both trumpet and Asiatic varieties, and they're known for their sweet fragrance. Lilies prefer full sun and moist, well-drained soil.

With so many beautiful options to choose from, it's hard to go wrong with any of these flowers for your home garden.

CHAPTER 2

Flower Farming for Beginners

For centuries, flowers have been cultivated for their beauty and fragrance. In the middle Ages, flower farms began to spring up in Europe, and by the 1600s, they were a common sight in the Netherlands. The Dutch were masters of horticulture, and they developed a wide variety of techniques for growing flowers. Thanks to their efforts, flower farms became increasingly popular in other parts of the world as well. Today, flower farms can be found on every continent, and they play an important role in the global economy. Flowers are still grown for their beauty and fragrance, but they also have a wide range of other uses. They are used in perfumes, cosmetics, and medicine, and they are also often given as gifts. Whatever their purpose, flowers will continue to bring joy to people all over the world for many years to come.

Flower farmers

A flower farmer is someone who grows flowers for a living. While that might seem like a simple enough definition, there's actually a lot more to it than meets the eye. For one thing, flower farmers need to have a keen understanding of horticulture. They need to know which flowers will flourish in which conditions, and how to care for them so that they stay healthy and beautiful. Additionally, flower farmers need to be skilled in the art of arranging flowers. After all, even the most stunning blooms will look lackluster if they're not arranged properly. But perhaps the most important quality that a flower farmer needs is passion. Growing flowers is a labor of love, and it takes a special person to do it well. So next time you admire a beautiful bouquet, take a moment to think about the hard-working flower farmer who made it possible.

Process for starting a flower farm

Farming flowers is no small feat, but it can be an incredibly rewarding experience. With a little bit of planning and some elbow grease, you can be well on your way to starting your very own flower farm.

- The first step is to choose the right location. You'll want to find a spot that gets plenty of sunlight and has well-drained soil.

- Once you've found the perfect spot, it's time to start prepping the land. This involves tasks like tilling the soil, removing rocks and debris, and adding compost.

- Next, you'll need to select the flowers you want to grow. Consider what types of flowers are in demand and what will grow well in your climate.

- Once you've made your selections, it's time to plant! Be sure to space the plants properly and give them enough water. With a little bit of care, your flower farm will be blooming in no time.

Flower farming Methods

Flower farming is no easy task - it takes knowing the ins and outs of flower biology, having a steady hand, and being patient enough to wait for blooms. The process begins with selecting the right location. Flower farmers need to take into account things like sunlight, drainage, and soil type when choosing a spot to set up shop. Once the perfect location has been found, it's time to start preparing the soil. This involves tilling, adding compost, and ensuring that the pH levels are just right. Then, the farmers can finally start planting their flowers. To ensure a good yield, they need to be careful about spacing the plants evenly and giving them enough room to grow. After all of this work, the flowers finally begin to bloom - and the real fun begins. Farmers need to constantly monitor their crop, deadheading flowers as necessary and keeping an eye out for pests. It's a lot of work, but at the end of the day, flower farmers get to enjoy the fruits (or rather, flowers) of their labor.

Flower farming methods vary according to the crop being grown, the climate, and the farmer's preference.

Some common methods include field production, greenhouse production, container production, and cut-flower production.

- Field production is often used for crops that require a lot of space, such as sunflowers. Field flower production is the process of growing flowers in open fields. This type of flower production is typically used for large-scale operations, such as commercial nurseries or florists. While field flower production requires more land than greenhouse production, it offers a number of benefits. For example, field flowers are exposed to natural light and weather conditions, which can help to toughen the plants and make them more resistant to pests and diseases. In addition, field flower production typically results in a higher yield per acre than greenhouse production. As a result, field flower production is an important part of the floral industry.

- Greenhouse production is ideal for crops that need to be

  protected from harsh weather conditions, such as daffodils.

  Flower production in greenhouses is a process that involves

  a lot of detail and precision. It takes skill to be able to

  control the environment inside the greenhouse in order to

  produce beautiful flowers. The first step in greenhouse

  flower production is to select the right variety of plants for

  the space and type of greenhouse you are working with.

  Then, you need to make sure that the plants have enough

light by positioning them close to the glass walls or roofs of the greenhouse. In terms of temperature, most flowers thrive in cooler temperatures, so it is important to keep the greenhouse within a range of 60-70 degrees Fahrenheit. Thirdly, the level of humidity inside the greenhouse should be monitored and kept at a moderate level - too much or too little moisture can damage delicate flowers. Finally, it is essential to fertilize regularly and provide good drainage in order to keep plants healthy. By following these steps, you can produce stunning flowers in a greenhouse environment.

- Container production is often used for crops that have a shallow root system, such as impatiens. Container flower production is a process that involves growing flowers in containers instead of in the ground. This method has many benefits, including the fact that it allows for more control over the environment in which the plants are grown. With container flower production, growers can control the amount of water and nutrients that plants receive, as well as the amount of light and heat they are exposed to. This precise control over growing conditions can lead to healthier plants and more vibrant flowers. In addition, container flower production is much less labor-intensive than traditional methods, making it a more efficient and cost-effective option for growers. As a result, it is no wonder that this method of flower production is becoming increasingly popular among growers of all levels of experience.

- Cut-flower production is used to grow flowers that will be harvested and sold fresh, such as roses. The term cut flowers refers to flowers that have been cut from their stems and are intended for use in a vase or other container. While many people enjoy growing cut flowers in their own gardens, others prefer to purchase them from a florist. Cut-flower production is a multimillion-dollar industry, and growers must contend with a wide range of challenges in order to produce high-quality blooms. Among the most important factors are climate, nutrition, and pest control. Additionally, growers must carefully time the harvest of their flowers in order to ensure that they will be fresh for the market. With proper care, however, it is possible to produce beautiful cut flowers that will bring enjoyment to people all over the world.

Each method has its own benefits and drawbacks, so it's important to choose the right method for the crop being grown.

Why flower farming is enjoyable

There are many reasons why flower farming can be enjoyable. It is a relatively easy way to get into agriculture. Unlike most crops, flowers can be grown in a wide range of climates, and they don't require a lot of land or specialized equipment. In addition, Flowers are typically sold by the stem, so there is no need to worry about packing or shipping bulk products. Because flowers are often given as gifts, there is a built-in market for your product. Flower farming can be a very rewarding experience. The sight of a freshly picked bouquet is enough to brighten anyone's day, and the satisfaction of knowing you grew those flowers yourself is priceless. So if you're looking for a fun and rewarding way to get into agriculture, consider flower farming.

CHAPTER 3

How to Start a Flower Farm Layout

Many people dream of starting their own flower farm. And why wouldn't they? Flowers are beautiful, and fragrant, and make the perfect addition to any home or garden. But where to start? The first step is to develop a basic layout for your farm. You'll need to choose a location that receives plenty of sunlight and has well-drained soil. Once you've found the perfect spot, you'll need to prepare the ground by tilling and raking it until it's smooth. Then, you can begin planting your flowers. Make sure to space them out properly so that they have room to grow. And that's it! With a little hard work and dedication, you'll have a thriving flower farm in no time.

A beautiful flower garden is the result of careful planning and forethought. By taking the time to map out a layout, you can create a cohesive design that is both aesthetically pleasing and functional. When planning your garden, be sure to take into account the size and shape of your space, as well as the amount of sunlight it receives. You'll also need to consider the needs of your plants, such as water and soil requirements. By taking all of these factors into account, you can create a flower garden that will thrive for years to come.

Before you can start a flower farm, you need to have a plan. This includes deciding what kind of flowers you want to grow, how much space you have to work with, and what type of equipment you'll need. You also need to think about the logistics of running a farm, such as how you'll market your flowers and how you'll ship them to customers. With a little bit of planning, starting a flower farm can be a rewarding and profitable endeavor.

Here are a few tips to get you started:

1. Decide what kind of flowers you want to grow: There are many different types of flowers that can be grown for profit, so it's important to choose the ones that are best suited for your climate and your market. Do some research and talk to other flower farmers to get an idea of which varieties are most popular and easiest to grow in your area.

2. Figure out how much space you have to work with: Flower farming requires quite a bit of space, so it's important to make sure you have enough land to support your operation.

In addition, you'll need space for storage, packaging, and shipping. If you're tight on space, consider growing flowers in containers or raised beds.

3. Get the right equipment: Flower farming requires some specialized equipment, such as greenhouses, irrigation systems, and potting soil mixers. You may be able to find used equipment at agricultural supply stores or online classified sites.

4. Develop a marketing plan: Once you've decided what kind of flowers you're going to grow and how you're going to grow them, it's time to start thinking about marketing. You'll need to develop a branding strategy and create promotional materials that will attract customers to your farm. You may also want to set up an online store or sell your flowers at local farmer's markets or florist's shops.

5. Create a shipping plan: If you're selling your flowers online or shipping them long distances, it's important to make sure they arrive fresh and undamaged. Pack your flowers

carefully using bubble wrap or shredded paper for padding, and ship them via overnight delivery service or a refrigerated trucking company.

Flower farm Layout

There are many different types of flower farm layouts. Some farmers prefer to grow their flowers in rows, while others use a more natural approach and allow the flowers to grow in a more free-flowing manner. Some farmers use a combination of both methods. No matter what type of layout you choose, there are a few things that you need to keep in mind. First, you need to make sure that the flowers have enough room to grow. Second, you need to ensure that the plants have enough sunlight. Lastly, you need to make sure that the plants have adequate drainage. If you can keep these three things in mind, then you will be well on your way to growing healthy and beautiful flowers.

There are a variety of flower farm layouts that growers can choose from, depending on the type of flower they want to grow and the amount of space they have available.

- One common layout is known as the field system, in which rows of crops are planted in long, straight lines. This system is often used for large-scale commercial production, as it allows growers to maximize their land usage and efficiently harvest their crops. However, it can also be used on smaller farms, provided that the rows are not too wide or too long.

- Another common layout is known as the bed system, in which crops are planted in raised beds. This system is often used in home gardens, as it allows for better drainage and easier weed control. It can also be adapted to larger farms, provided that the beds are not too large or too close together.

No matter what type of layout you choose, there are a few things to keep in mind in order to ensure a successful harvest. First, make sure that your rows are spaced evenly and that your crop spacing is consistent. Second, ensure that your beds are level and free of debris. Finally, make sure to water your plants regularly and fertilize them according to their needs. By following these simple tips, you can create a healthy and productive flower farm that will provide you with beautiful blooms for years to come.

Making a flower field

To make a flower field, you'll need a lot of space, some good soil, and a variety of perennial flowers. First, till the soil and remove any rocks or debris. Then, add some organic matter to help the flowers thrive. Next, choose your flowers. Annuals will need to be replanted every year, but perennials will come back on their own. Be sure to plant a mix of tall and short flowers, as well as those that bloom at different times of the year. Finally, water regularly and fertilize according to the needs of your particular plants. With a little care, you'll soon have a beautiful flower field that will bring you joy for years to come.

If you're looking to add a splash of color to your life, then planting a flower field is a great way to do it. But how exactly do you go about creating a beautiful flower field?

Here are a few tips:

1. Choose the right location: You'll need a spot that gets plenty of sunlight and has well-drained soil. Avoid low-lying areas where water can collect, as this can lead to problems with rot and fungal diseases.

2. Prepare the soil: Once you've found the perfect spot, it's time to get your hands dirty. Break up any clumps of soil and remove any weeds or other plants that might compete with your flowers for nutrients.

3. Choose the right plants: Not all flowers are created equal when it comes to fields. Look for varieties that are quick-

growing and have a long bloom period. Be sure to space the plants properly so they have room to grow and spread out.

4. Water regularly: Flowers need lots of water, especially during the hot summer months. Keep an eye on the forecast and water your field accordingly. If possible, set up an irrigation system to help make things easier.

5. Deadhead as needed: Once the flowers start blooming, you'll need to deadhead them regularly to encourage new growth. This simply means removing spent blossoms so the plant can focus its energy on producing new ones.

Life is like a flower field, full of beauty but also requires some time to reach its full potential! By following these tips, you can enjoy all the colorful splendor of a flower field without all the hassle.

Designing a flower pattern

Planting a flower pattern may seem like a daunting task, but with a little planning, it can be easily accomplished.

If you're looking to add a splash of color to your garden, planting a flower pattern is a great way to do it. There are a few things to keep in mind when you're creating your design.

- First, choose a color scheme that you love: You can go for a monochromatic look with different shades of the same color, or mix and match different hues for a more eclectic feel.

- Plan: Once you've decided on your colors, it's time to start planning your design. Once you have your plan, it's time to get started planting! Begin by digging holes for each of your flowers, making sure that they are spaced evenly apart. Then, simply drop in your plants and cover them with soil. Water them well and watch them grow! In no time at all, you'll have a beautiful flower pattern that will add life to your garden.

- Decide on the overall shape of the pattern: Once you have a general idea of the shape, you can begin planning the individual plants. When selecting plants, it is important to consider their mature size, as well as their growing habits. You can plant a flower pattern by using a simple method called the drop and zigzag method. First, you will need to find a straight line that you can use as a guide, such as a sidewalk or a driveway. Then, starting at one end of the line, drop a flower seed every few inches. Once you have dropped all of the seeds on one side of the line, zigzag back and forth across the line, dropping seeds as you go. When you reach the other end of the line, you should have a beautiful pattern of flowers. This method is simple and efficient, and it will help you achieve stunning results.

- Bloom: You will also need to choose plants that will bloom at different times of the year so that the pattern will remain colorful for many months. Once you have selected the plants, you can begin laying them out in the desired pattern. Be sure to allow enough space between each plant, so that they will have room to grow. When you are satisfied with the layout, you can start planting. Be careful not to disturb the roots of the plants as you dig your holes, and be sure to give them plenty of water after planting. With a little care and attention, your flower pattern will soon be blooming beautifully!

Organizing a flower garden

A well-organized flower garden can bring both beauty and order to your outdoor space. But how do you go about creating such a garden? The first step is to choose a layout that suits your needs. If you have a large space, you may want to consider a traditional design with rows of flowers separated by paths.

Any gardener will tell you that organization is key when it comes to growing flowers. After all, even the most beautiful blooms can quickly become overgrown and unruly if they're not given the proper care. For those who are looking to add a touch of floral beauty to their yard, here are a few tips on how to organize a flower garden.

First, take into account the amount of space you have available. This will help you determine how many and what type of plants you'll be able to accommodate. For smaller spaces, a more informal design may be best. Once you have chosen a layout, it's time to select your plants.

Decide on a color palette. This will help you create a cohesive look for your garden. Once you've decided on these basic elements, you can begin planning your flower garden. Just remember to keep it organized, so that your yard remains both beautiful and manageable. When choosing plants, it's important to consider the size, shape, and color of each one. You'll also want to make sure that they are compatible with each other and will bloom at the same time.

Next, consider the amount of sunlight the area receives throughout the day. This will determine which flowers will thrive in your garden. After you've selected your plants, it's time to start planting! Be sure to dig holes that are twice as wide as the roots of your plants and loosen the soil before placing them in the ground. Once your plants are in the ground, water them well and add mulch to help retain moisture. With a little care and attention, your garden will soon be blooming!

Garden layout

The garden layout is the organization of the different areas in the garden. This includes the types of plants that are grown in each area, how they are arranged, and the paths and walkways that lead through the garden. A well-designed layout can help to create a sense of order and harmony in the garden, while also providing functionality and practicality. The most popular layouts include traditional, cottage, and formal designs. Each of these has its own unique benefits and drawbacks, so it is important to choose a layout that best suits your individual needs. Regardless of which layout you choose, remember that the key to a successful garden is to start with a good plan.

One of the most important things to consider when designing a garden is the layout. The layout should be planned in such a way that it makes the most efficient use of space and allows for easy movement between plants. It is also important to consider the amount of sunlight that each area of the garden will receive. This will dictate which plants will thrive in which location. For example, vegetables generally need full sun, while shade-loving plants such as ferns can prosper in areas that receive little direct sunlight. By carefully planning the layout of the garden, it is possible to create a beautiful and functional space that meets all of your gardening needs.

CHAPTER 4

Flower farming for profit

Flower farming is a fast-growing industry with immense profit potential. In fact, according to the Society of American Florists, the average return on investment for a flower farm is between 50 and 150 percent. And that's not even counting the numerous intangible benefits, such as the joy of working with nature and the satisfaction of bringing beauty into the world.

Of course, like any business venture, starting a flower farm requires careful planning and a bit of start-up capital. But if you're passionate about flowers and have a green thumb, it could be the perfect way to turn your passion into profit. So what are you waiting for? Start your own flower farm today!

Any business can be profitable if it is managed correctly and the flower farming business is no different. One important aspect of flowers that must be taken into account is the fact that they are perishable items. This means that there is a time limit on when they must be sold and if they are not sold in time, they will wilt and die. Because of this, it is important to have a plan for how the flowers will be distributed and sold. One option is to sell them at farmer's markets or local florists. Another option is to create arrangements and sell them online. Whichever route you choose, it is important to price the flowers correctly in order to make a profit. If managed correctly, the flower farming business can be quite profitable.

If you're looking for a way to make some extra money, you might want to consider flower farming. Yes, that's right - flower farming! It may not be the first thing that comes to mind when you think of making money, but it can actually be quite profitable. There are a number of ways to make money in flower farming, from selling bouquets to renting out your space for weddings and other events. And the best part is that it can be a very rewarding experience. Not only will you get to enjoy the beauty of your flowers, but you'll also get the satisfaction of knowing that you're helping to make someone's day just a little bit brighter. So if you're looking for a fun and profitable way to make some extra money, flower farming just might be the perfect option for you!

If you're thinking about starting a small farm, you may be wondering if flower farming is profitable. The answer is, it depends. Flower farming can be a very lucrative business, but it takes a lot of hard work and dedication to make it successful.

Here are a few things you need to know about flower farming for profit:

First, you need to have a market for your flowers. You can sell them wholesale to florists or directly to customers at farmers' markets or through a flower delivery business. It's important to understand your market and what they are willing to pay for your flowers.

Second, you need to grow a variety of flowers that are in demand. You'll need to do some research to find out what kinds of flowers are popular in your area and how much they cost.

Third, you need to be able to grow high-quality flowers. This means having the right soil, using the right fertilizers, and providing the plants with the proper amount of water and sunlight. It takes practice and patience to get it right, but it's essential if you want to have happy customers who keep coming back for more.

Fourth, you need to have good business sense. This means knowing how to price your flowers so that you make a profit, keeping track of your expenses, and marketing your business effectively. If you can do all of these things, then you can be successful at flower farming for profit.

Most profitable Flowers

While many flowers are grown for their beauty, some varieties are also prized for their value as crop plants. Among the most popular and profitable flowers for farmers are roses, tulips, lilies, and chrysanthemums. Each of these flowers has a long history of cultivation, and they continue to be in high demand among florists and gardeners alike. While all four of these flowers can be quite lucrative, roses are often considered the most profitable, due to their relatively high price point and strong market demand. With proper care and marketing, farmers can expect to earn a healthy profit from growing any of these flowers.

According to industry experts, the most profitable type of flower farming is actually daffodil farming. Daffodils are not only relatively easy to grow, but they also have a long flowering season and a wide range of colors and shapes. As a result, they are in high demand among florists and other customers. In addition, daffodils are relatively resistant to pests and disease, meaning that they require less time and money to maintain. For these reasons, daffodil farming is often considered one of the most lucrative types of flower farming.

Most people think of flower farming as a hobby, something done in one's spare time to generate a little extra income. However, there are those who have turned flower farming into a profitable business. The key to success is to choose the right crop and to grow it in an area with a high demand. For example, roses are a popular choice for flower farmers because they can be sold year-round and fetches a high price. In contrast, daisies are less expensive and have a shorter shelf life, making them less profitable. Another important factor to consider is the climate. Roses require a warm climate in order to thrive, so they are typically grown in places like California or Florida. If you want to be successful at flower farming, you need to do your research and choose the right crop for your location and market. With the right planning, you can turn flower farming into a thriving business.

The good profit margin for flowers

When it comes to flowers, there is no one-size-fits-all answer to the question of what constitutes a good profit margin. Different types of flowers fetch different prices, and even within a given type of flower, there can be significant variation in price points depending on factors like quality and availability. For example, roses are typically priced higher than daisies, and long-stemmed roses will generally command a higher price than shorter-stemmed varieties. In general, though, most growers aim for a profit margin of 50% or more on their flowers. This allows them to cover their costs while still delivering a product that is competitively priced in the market. Of course, in order to achieve such a margin, growers must carefully manage their production costs and ensure that their flowers are of the highest quality. But for those who are able to do so, flowers can be a very lucrative business indeed.

As anyone who has ever tried to sell flowers knows, it can be a tough business. Flowers are delicate and perishable, which means they have a limited shelf life. They also require a great deal of care and attention, both in the field and in the floral shop. As a result, flower prices can be quite high, and profit margins can be slim. So what is a good profit margin for flowers? The answer depends on a number of factors, including the type of flower, the time of year, and the local market conditions. In general, though, most flower growers aim for a profit margin of 20-30%. In some cases, growers may be able to get by with a smaller margin, while in others they may need to make do with a larger one. But 20-30% is a good target to aim for. The markup on flowers is typically only 50-100%, it's clear that there's room for a healthy profit margin. Of course, there are always exceptions to the rule, and in some cases, it may be possible to earn a higher profit margin. However, as a general guideline, 20-30% is a good target to aim for when selling flowers.

Flower farm business plan

Before you can start raking in the dough from your very own flower farm, you'll need to put together a solid business plan. While this may sound like a daunting task, it's not as difficult as it seems.

Any business plan worth it's salt will address the four main components of a successful business: your product, your market, your team, and your financials. When it comes to starting a flower farm, there are a few things you'll need to keep in mind. First, what type of flowers do you want to grow? There are many different types of flowers that can be grown commercially, so you'll need to choose the ones that are best suited for your climate and soil type. You'll also need to consider the needs of your target market. Who are you selling your flowers to? Wholesale buyers? Retail florists? Event planners? Once you've decided on your product and market, it's time to put together your team. Are you going to be running the farm on your own, or do you have partners? What type of skills and experience will they bring to the table? Finally, you'll need to create financial projections for your business. How much will it cost to get started? How much can you realistically expect to earn in revenues? These are just a few of the questions you'll need to answer in your flower farm business plan. By taking the time to develop a well-rounded business plan, you'll increase your chances of success exponentially.

The first step to starting any business is creating a business plan. This document will outline your business goals, strategies, and how you plan on achieving them. While it may seem like a daunting task, a little planning can go a long way. Here are a few tips on how to create a flower farm business plan:

1. Define your business goals: What do you hope to achieve with your flower farm? Do you want to be a wholesale supplier, operate a retail store, or provide flowers for special events? Once you know your objectives, you can start developing your strategies.

2. Research the market: Take some time to learn about the flower industry. Who are your potential customers? What do they want? How much are they willing to pay? This information will help you determine what products and services to offer and how to price them competitively.

3. Develop a marketing plan: How will you let potential customers know about your business? Will you advertise in local newspapers or online? Do you plan on participating in trade shows or setting up a booth at community events? Your marketing plan should be designed to reach your target audience and promote your products or services effectively.

4. Create a financial plan: This will include an estimate of your start-up costs, operating expenses, and projected revenue. It's important to be realistic when creating your financial projections - remember that most businesses take time to generate profits.

By following these tips, you'll be well on your way to creating a successful flower farm business plan.

Cost of starting a flower farm

Starting a flower farm can be a relatively inexpensive endeavor, or it can cost a pretty penny - it all depends on the size and scope of your operation. If you're just growing a few flowers in your backyard to sell at the farmer's market, you can get by with just a small investment in seeds, soil, and basic gardening supplies. However, if you're planning to start a large-scale commercial operation, the costs can quickly add up. You'll need to purchase land, build greenhouses or other structures, invest in irrigation and farming equipment, and hire staff. In addition, you'll need to factor in the costs of marketing and advertising to make sure your flowers are flying off the shelves. So, while the cost of starting a flower farm varies depending on your plans, one thing is for sure - it's not going to be cheap. But with a little hard work (and maybe a lot of money), you can make your dream of becoming a professional flower farmer a reality.

CHAPTER 5

How to Start a Rose Flower Farm

Roses are one of the most popular flowers in the world, and they're known for their delicate beauty and stunning blooms. But what many people don't realize is that roses can be quite finicky when it comes to their growing conditions. In order to thrive, roses need full sun, well-drained soil, and regular watering. However, even with all of these things, roses can still be susceptible to pests and diseases. As a result, growing roses is not for the faint of heart. But for those who are willing to put in the effort, the rewards are definitely worth it. After all, there's nothing quite like a freshly cut rose from your own garden.

Flowers are one of the most popular gifts to give and receive. Roses, in particular, are associated with love, appreciation, and congratulations. As a result, there is always a demand for fresh roses. One way to take advantage of this demand is to start a rose flower farm.

There are a few things you will need in order to get started. First, you will need a plot of land where you can grow your roses. You will also need to obtain some rose bushes or plants. These can be purchased from a nursery or online. Once you have your plants, you will need to prepare the soil. This involves adding organic matter and making sure the pH is correct. Then, you will need to plant your roses and water them regularly.

Farming roses is no small feat. It takes a lot of time, patience, and effort to successfully cultivate these beautiful flowers. However, if you're up for the challenge, starting a rose farm can be a rewarding experience.

Here are a few tips to get you started:

1. First, you'll need to choose the right location. Roses prefer well-drained soil and full sun exposure.

2. Next, you'll need to start preparing the soil. This includes adding organic matter and amendments to create the perfect environment for your roses to thrive.

3. Once the soil is ready, it's time to plant your roses. Make sure to space them out properly so they have room to grow.

4. After planting, you'll need to water your roses regularly and mulch around the base of each plant to help retain moisture.

5. Finally, you'll need to prune your roses regularly to encourage new growth and prevent them from getting too leggy.

With a little bit of hard work, you can create a thriving rose farm that will provide you with years of enjoyment.

Rose Farming

Rose farming is the cultivation of roses. It involves the growing of roses for commercial purposes, as well as for use in rose oil and rose water production. Rose farming began in Europe during the 18th century, and by the 19th century, it had spread to countries such as America, China, and Japan. Today, roses are grown in many different parts of the world, and there are over 150 varieties of roses that are commercially available. The most popular types of roses include Hybrid Tea Roses, Floribunda Roses, and Miniature Roses. Rose farming requires a great deal of care and attention, as roses are delicate flowers that need to be given the proper amount of sunlight, water, and nutrients in order to flourish. With the right care, however, roses can be beautiful and fragrant additions to any garden.

Rose farming is the cultivation of roses for their beautiful flowers. Roses have been grown for centuries for their aesthetic appeal, and today they are one of the most popular flowers in the world. Rose farmers must have a keen eye for detail, as each rose bush must be individually cared for to produce the best blooms. This includes regular pruning and fertilizing, as well as ensuring that the plants have enough water. Rose farming can be a demanding but rewarding profession, and those who are successful in this field can take great pride in their handiwork.

Rose farming is not only about producing pretty flowers, it is also about developing new and improved varieties of roses. By cross-pollinating different types of roses, farmers can create roses with unique colors, shapes, and scents. Some of the most popular varieties of roses were created in this way, and new varieties are being developed all the time. For those who love roses, there is always something new to discover in the world of rose farming.

Suitable Temperature for Roses

Roses are one of the most popular flowers in the world, and they come in a wide range of colors, shapes, and sizes. While all roses need sunlight to grow, the amount of sun they need can vary depending on the variety. Some roses, such as hybrid teas and grandifloras, require full sun in order to produce an abundance of blooms. Other varieties, such as floribundas and climbing roses, can tolerate more shade and may even flower better if they receive some protection from the midday sun. In general, roses need at least six hours of direct sunlight each day in order to thrive. However, if you live in an area with very hot summers, it's best to provide some afternoon shade for your roses to prevent them from getting too much heat.

When it comes to the temperature that rose plants can survive, it really depends on the type of rose plant. For instance, some varieties can handle temperatures as low as -30 degrees Fahrenheit, while others can only tolerate temperatures as high as 50 degrees Fahrenheit. In general, however, most rose plants can survive temperatures between 40 and 50 degrees Fahrenheit. So, if you're hoping to grow roses in your garden, you'll need to make sure that you choose a variety that is appropriate for your climate. With so many different varieties to choose from, there's sure to be a rose plant that can thrive in your neck of the woods.

Though roses are often associated with warmth and sunshine, they can actually survive in a wide range of temperatures. Most varieties can tolerate temperatures as low as -10 degrees Fahrenheit, and some even withstand brief periods of colder weather. In fact, it is the fluctuations in temperature that are most likely to damage rose plants. For example, when temperatures rise quickly during the day and then drop sharply at night, the plant's cell walls can break down, causing the leaves to wilt. To protect against this, gardeners should water their rose plants regularly and mulch around the base of the plant to help insulate the roots. With a little care, roses can thrive in both hot and cold climates.

Planting roses from cuttings

Anyone who has ever attempted to grow roses from cuttings knows that it can be a bit of a hit-or-miss proposition. However, with a little patience and the following tips, you can increase your chances of success.

First, choose healthy, disease-free rose stems that are about six inches long. Cut the stem at an angle just below a leaf node, then remove all but the top two leaves. Dip the cutting in rooting hormone, then plant it in a well-draining potting mix. Water well and place the pot in a bright location out of direct sunlight. Keep the soil moist, but not soggy, and within a few weeks, you should see new growth. With a little care and attention, you can soon have a beautiful rose bush of your own.

Roses are one of the most popular flowers in the world, and they can make a beautiful addition to any garden. If you're thinking about planting roses, you may be wondering how to get started. One option is to plant roses from cuttings.

Here's what you need to know about planting roses from cuttings:

- First, choose a healthy rose bush to take your cuttings from. Cut a 6-8 inch stem from the bush, making sure to include several leaf nodes. These nodes are where the roots will grow from, so it's important to include them in your cutting.

- Next, dip the cut end of the stem in the rooting hormone. This will help encourage root growth. Plant the stem in a pot filled with moistened potting mix, and make sure that at least two leaf nodes are buried beneath the soil. Water well and place the pot in a bright location out of direct sunlight.

- Keep an eye on your cutting, and water as needed to keep the soil moist but not soggy. After a few weeks, you should see new growth appearing at the leaf nodes. Once your cutting has rooted and begun to grow, you can transplant it into your garden.

- Once all of the cuttings are planted, water them well and cover the tray with a sheet of plastic. Place the tray in a bright, warm location out of direct sunlight. Keep an eye on the cuttings, and water them as needed to keep the soil moist but not soggy. In four to six weeks, you should see new growth emerging from the cuttings - at which point you can transplant them into individual pots or your garden bed. Now all you have to do is sit back and enjoy your beautiful roses!

With a little patience and care, you can successfully grow roses from cuttings. Cuttings are a great option if you want to start a rose garden without spending a lot of money on plants. Give it a try and see for yourself!

Duration of rose cuttings rooting in water

Rose cuttings typically take about four to eight weeks to root in water. The amount of time it takes will depend on the type of rose and the conditions under which the cutting is grown. For example, cuttings that are taken from older roses tend to root more quickly than those taken from younger plants. In addition, cuttings that are grown in warm, humid conditions will typically root faster than those grown in cooler, drier conditions. However, regardless of the type of rose or the growing conditions, all cuttings will eventually develop roots if they are kept in water for long enough. So if you're patient, you'll eventually see your rose cuttings take root and begin to grow.

A rose cutting is a young shoot that has been cut from a mature plant and can be used to propagate a new rose bush. Rose cuttings are typically taken from late spring to early summer, when the plants are actively growing. The best way to take a rose cutting is to choose a healthy shoot that is about 6-8 inches long. Make sure to use sharp pruning shears or a knife to avoid damaging the plant.

Once you have cut the shoot, remove the lower leaves and dip the end in rooting hormone. Then, place the cutting in a glass of water and put it in a bright spot out of direct sunlight. Within 2-3 weeks, you should see roots beginning to form. Once the roots are about an inch long, you can transplant the cutting into the soil. With proper care, your new rose bush should begin blooming within 2-3 years.

Time it takes for roses to grow roots

One of the most common questions asked by new gardeners is "How long does it take for roses to grow roots?" The answer, unfortunately, is not a simple one. The speed of root growth depends on a number of factors, including the type of rose, the growing conditions, and the stage of growth. For example, young seedlings will usually develop roots more quickly than mature plants. Additionally, warm weather and ample moisture will encourage root growth, while cold temperatures and drought can slow it down. As a general rule of thumb, it takes about six weeks for roses to develop a good root system. However, patience is key when growing roses, and even the most experienced gardeners sometimes find themselves waiting a bit longer for their plants to take root.

CHAPTER 6

Backyard Flower Farm

A backyard flower farm may sound like a lot of work, but it can be a fun and rewarding experience. Not only will you have a beautiful garden to enjoy, but you'll also be able to sell your flowers at farmer's markets or even start your own flower-arranging business. The key to success is to start small and focus on just a few varieties of flowers. Then, once you've gotten the hang of things, you can gradually expand your operation. With a little planning and some hard work, you can turn your backyard into a thriving flower farm.

Have you ever considered starting a backyard flower farm? It's a great way to get outdoors, enjoy some fresh air, and get your hands dirty. Plus, there's nothing quite like the satisfaction of watching your flowers grow. Here are a few things to keep in mind if you're thinking of starting a backyard flower farm.

First, decide what kind of flowers you want to grow. Do you want to grow roses? Sunflowers? Daisies? There are many different types of flowers to choose from, so it's important to pick the ones that you're most interested in.

Second, make sure you have the right tools for the job. You'll need things like soil, fertilizer, watering cans, and gardening gloves. You may also want to invest in some plant stakes and netting to help support your plants as they grow.

Third, create a planting schedule. This will help you keep track of when to sow your seeds, when to thin out your plants, and when to harvest your blooms. A planting schedule will also help you make the most of your space by ensuring that you always have something in bloom.

Don't forget to enjoy the process! Growing flowers can be a lot of work, but it can also be very rewarding. So take your time, savor the moments, and let yourself be happy with every Bloom!

Flower farm equipments

Any farmer will tell you that equipment is an essential part of running a successful farm. The same is true for flower farms. From seed trays and transplant carts to hoop houses and pesticide sprayers, there is a wide range of equipment that can help flower farmers optimize their operations. Let's take a closer look at some of the most commonly used flower farm equipment.

- One of the most important pieces of equipment for any flower farmer is a seed trays and transplant cart. This type of equipment is used to sow seeds and then transport them to the planting area. Seed trays come in a variety of sizes and can be made from different materials, such as plastic or metal. Transplant carts are typically used to move larger plants, such as shrubs or trees. They can be equipped with wheels or tracks, depending on the size and weight of the plants being moved.

- Another essential piece of flower farm equipment is a hoop house. Hoop houses are typically made from PVC pipe or metal tubing and are covered with a transparent material, such as polyethylene film. They provide protection from the elements, including wind, rain, and snow. Hoop houses can also help regulate temperature and humidity levels, making them ideal for propagating plants or starting seedlings early in the season.

- Pesticide sprayers are another important piece of equipment for flower farmers. Pesticide sprayers are used to apply herbicides, insecticides, and fungicides to crops. They come in a variety of sizes and can be equipped with different types of nozzles, depending on the type of pesticide being applied. Most pesticide sprayers have a backpack-style design, which allows farmers to apply pesticides without having to carry heavy tanks or containers.

- One of the most important pieces of equipment for any flower farmer is a greenhouse. Greenhouses provide a controlled environment for plants, protecting them from extreme temperatures and weather conditions. They can also help to extend the growing season, allowing you to get a head start on the competition.

- If you're planning on growing cut flowers, then you'll also need a walk-in cooler. Cut flowers have a very short shelf life, so it's important to keep them cool and fresh. Walk-in coolers provide the perfect environment for storing cut flowers, keeping them hydrated, and delaying wilting.

- Other essential pieces of equipment for flower farmers include irrigation systems, plant supports, and row coverings. These pieces of equipment help to ensure that your plants are getting the water and nutrients they need to thrive. With the right equipment, you can set your flower farm up for success.

There is a wide range of equipment that can be used on flower farms. Seed trays and transplant carts help farmers sow seeds and move plants around the farm. Hoop houses provide protection from the elements and can also help regulate temperature and humidity levels. Pesticide sprayers allow farmers to apply herbicides, insecticides, and fungicides without having to carry heavy containers or tanks around the farm. By using this type of equipment, flower farmers can optimize their operations and produce healthy plants year-round.

Starting your backyard flower farm

A well-tended lawn can play an essential role in preventing soil erosion. Grassroots help to hold the soil in place, and the dense network of blades helps to deflect wind and water. In addition, lawns help to slow down the flow of rainwater, giving the ground a chance to absorb the water before it runs off. As a result, a well-tended lawn can play an essential role in preventing soil erosion. Starting a backyard flower farm may seem like a daunting task, but with a little planning, it can be surprisingly easy. The first step is to choose the right location. Look for an area that gets plenty of sunlight and has well-drained soil. Once you've found the perfect spot, it's time to start planting. Select a variety of flowers that will bloom at different times of the year, so you'll always have something in bloom. Be sure to plant enough flowers to allow for proper spacing between each plant. After your flowers are in the ground, water them regularly and fertilize them according to package directions. With a little care and attention, your backyard flower farm will soon be in full bloom!

A backyard can be the perfect place to start a flower farm. With a little planning, you can create a productive space that will provide you with beautiful blooms year after year.

One of the most important considerations for a successful flower farm is sunlight. Make sure to choose a location that gets plenty of sun throughout the day. This will ensure that your flowers have the energy they need to grow and bloom. Another important factor is soil quality. Flower farms need rich, well-drained soil in order to produce healthy plants. If your backyard does not have ideal soil, you can improve it by adding organic matter such as compost or manure.

Once you have chosen the perfect location and prepared the soil, it is time to select the flowers you want to grow. Consider the climate in your area and choose varieties that are well-suited to your conditions. With a little care and attention, you can create a productive backyard flower farm that will provide you with years of enjoyment.

CHAPTER 7

Sunflower Farm

A sunflower farm is a great way to add some beautiful blooms to your landscape. But before you can enjoy the fruits of your labor, there are a few things you need to do to get started.

If you've ever wanted to grow your own sunflowers, then a sunflower farm may be the perfect business for you. Sunflowers are easy to grow and care for, and they make a beautiful addition to any landscape. Plus, sunflower seeds are a healthy and delicious snack that can be enjoyed by people of all ages.

Sunflower seeds are best planted in early spring after the last frost has passed. You'll need to choose a sunny spot in your yard or garden where the sunflowers will have plenty of room to grow. Once the seeds have been planted, water them regularly and keep an eye out for weeds. Sunflowers are relatively low-maintenance plants, but they will need to be fertilized every few weeks during the growing season.

As the sunflowers begin to bloom, you can either sell them at a farmer's market or cut them yourself and arrange them into bouquets. Sunflower bouquets make beautiful gifts or decoration for weddings and other special occasions. You can also sell sunflower seeds by the pound as a tasty and healthy snack food.

With a little planning and care, you can have a thriving sunflower farm that brings joy to everyone who sees it - including yourself!

You'll need to find a sunny spot in your yard that gets at least six hours of direct sunlight each day. Then, you'll need to till the soil to a depth of about eight inches. Once the soil is loose and evenly textured, you can start planting your sunflower seeds. To ensure that your seeds have the best chance of germinating, plant them about an inch deep and six inches apart.

Once your sunflower seeds have been planted, all you need to do is water them regularly and wait for them to grow. In just a few weeks, you'll have towering sunflowers adding some much-needed color to your yard. And with a little care and patience, you can enjoy fresh sunflowers for years to come.

Overview of sunflower

Sunflowers are one of the most popular flowers in the world. With their large, vibrant blooms, they add a touch of cheerfulness to any garden. But did you know that sunflowers are also a type of plant? In fact, they belong to the Asteraceae family, which includes daisies, asters, and chrysanthemums. Sunflowers are native to North America, and they have been cultivated for centuries. Today, there are over 60 species of sunflower, and they come in a wide range of colors, including yellow, red, orange, and even blue.

Whether you're looking for a pop of color or a simple green leafy plant, sunflowers are a great option.

Helianthus annuus, otherwise known as the common sunflower, is an annual plant in the family Asteraceae, native to the Americas. Growing to a height of 2.5 m (8.2 ft), it bears a large head of flower rays in shades of yellow, gold, orange, and brown with a dark disc at the center. The plant has a thick, hairy stem which supports the flower head and leaves. The leaves are large and oval-shaped, with serrated edges. This annual plant is native to America, and can grow up to a whopping 8 feet tall! But it's best known for its large head of beautiful flowers, which come in all sorts of Yellow, gold, orange, and brown shades. And at the center of each sunflower is a dark disc. Pretty cool, right? But wait - there's more! The sunflower's stem is also pretty unique. It's thick and hairy (not something you usually say about plants!), and it does a great job of supporting the flower head and leaves. Speaking of leaves: they're usually big and oval-shaped with serrated edges. All in all, the sunflower is a pretty amazing plant - and one that definitely deserves a closer look!

According to the World Atlas, the largest producer of sunflowers is Russia, followed by Ukraine and Argentina. That's no surprise when you consider that sunflowers are native to the region around the Black Sea. The flower was first cultivated by the ancient Greeks, who used it as a decoration in temples and tombs. Sunflowers later became a symbol of hope and faith during dark times in Russian history. Today, the vibrant blooms are cherished around the world for their beauty and versatility. The flavorful seeds are popular in snacks and bird feeders, while the oil is used in cooking and cosmetics. With such a long history and wide range of uses, it's no wonder that sunflowers continue to bloom in popularity.

The sunflower is a beautiful plant that has captivated people for centuries. Though most commonly associated with warmth and happiness, the sunflower can also symbolize loyalty and strength. This fascinating plant gets its name from its large, bright flowers, which resemble the sun. Sunflowers are native to North America, but they have been cultivated around the world for their striking appearance and edible seeds. The sunflower is an annual plant, which means that it completes its life cycle in one growing season. During that time, the plant grows from a small seedling to a towering bush covered in flowers. Each flower head is actually made up of hundreds of smaller flowers, called florets. The sunflower is a delightful plant that brings beauty and enjoyment to people all over the globe.

Where sunflowers grow best

Today, sunflowers are grown in many parts of the world, but they thrive in warm, sunny climates. In the United States, sunflowers are typically planted in late May or early June. They prefer well-drained soil and full sunlight. Given their preference for warm weather, sunflowers are often grown as annuals in cooler climates. However, in tropical regions, they can be grown as perennials. Sunflowers are relatively easy to care for and require very little maintenance. Once they are established, they will flower continuously throughout the summer months. With their bright yellow petals and cheery disposition, sunflowers are a welcome addition to any garden.

While sunflowers are often associated with sunny days and warm weather, sunflowers actually prefer cooler temperatures. They also need full sun and well-drained soil. In terms of climate, sunflowers are best suited for growing in temperate regions. However, they can also be grown in subtropical and tropical areas if they're given enough water. So whether you live in the desert or the mountains, there's a good chance you can grow beautiful sunflowers in your own backyard.

Sunflower growth time

Are you looking to add a splash of yellow to your garden? Then consider planting sunflowers! These cheerful flowers are not only easy to grow, but they also make for excellent cut flowers. Most sunflower varieties will be ready to harvest in just two to three months.

Some varieties, such as the Dwarf Sunflower, will reach maturity in as little as 60 days. Other varieties, such as the Giant Sunflower, can take up to 120 days. But no matter which variety you choose, you can be sure that your sunflowers will bring a smile to your face.

A sunflower needs about six to eight weeks of warm weather to grow from a seed to a mature plant. During that time, the sunflower will pass through several stages of growth. The first stage is when the seed germinates and a small seedling emerges from the ground. The second stage is when the plant begins to produce leaves and put down roots. The third stage is when the plant starts to produce a stem and buds. And finally, the fourth stage is when the plant blooms and produces flowers. Once the sunflower blooms, it will continue to produce flowers for several weeks before its petals start to fall off and its life cycle comes to an end. However, during that time, the sunflower will provide food and shelter for many different types of wildlife, including bees, birds, and butterflies. In that way, even after its death, the sunflower continues to give back to the earth.

Sunflowers are relatively easy to grow. Just be sure to plant them in full sun and give them plenty of room to spread their roots.

Farming sunflower seeds

Let's be honest, when most of us think about farming, we don't think about sunflower seeds. We think about wheat or corn or soybeans. But the fact is, sunflower seeds are an important crop in many parts of the world. In the United States, for example, sunflower seeds are grown in states like Colorado, Kansas, and North Dakota. And while the process of growing sunflower seeds may seem relatively simple, there's actually a lot that goes into it.

For starters, sunflower seeds need to be planted in well-drained soil that has been amended with plenty of organic matter. They also need full sun - at least six hours per day - and regular watering. Once the plants have sprouted and begun to grow, they will need to be thinned so that they are spaced about 12 inches apart. This ensures that each plant has enough room to reach its full potential. Once the plants have flowered and the petals have begun to fall off, the seed heads need to be harvested. This is typically done by cutting the plant at the base and hanging it upside down so that the seeds can be shaken out. With a little care and attention, anyone can enjoy a beautiful sunflower crop.

Sunflowers are one of the most popular flowers in the world, and their seeds are cherished for their nutritional value. The process begins with a field of blooming sunflowers. Once the flowers have reached maturity, they are cut down and gathered into bundles. The bundles are then taken to a thresher, where the seeds are extracted from the flower heads. The seeds are then cleaned and sorted before being packaged for sale. The entire process is quite fascinating, and it's no wonder that sunflower seeds are such a beloved treat.

Sunflower seeds are planted in the spring, typically in April or May. Farmers will sow the seeds in rows, and then thin out the plants once they've germinated. The thinned-out plants are typically transplanted to another location so that they have more room to grow. Once the plants have blossomed, the flowers will be harvested and the seeds will be extracted. The seeds will then be cleaned and sorted before being packaged and shipped to buyers.

So next time you're crunching down on a handful of sunflower seeds, take a moment to think about all the hard work that went into getting them to your plate. Who knows, maybe you'll even develop a newfound appreciation for these little Seeds!

Sunflower water Requirement

Sunflowers are one of the sunniest, most cheerful flowers around. They are easy to grow and make a great addition to any garden. Sunflowers are actually quite drought-tolerant, and they can actually suffer if they get too much water. Overwatering can cause the roots to rot, and the plant may become stunted or even die. So, if you're looking for a low-maintenance flower that doesn't require a lot of water, sunflowers are a great option. Just be sure to plant them in well-drained soil and give them plenty of sunshine.

During the growing season, sunflowers should be watered about once a week, making sure to moisten the soil to a depth of six inches. More water may be necessary during periods of extended drought. In addition to regular watering, adding mulch to the soil around sunflowers can help to conserve moisture and prevent weed growth. With the right care, sunflowers will continue to bring smiles all summer long.

Sunflowers are actually quite drought tolerant and can survive on very little water. Their deep roots help them to access underground water reserves, and their thick leaves protect their delicate flowers from the harsh rays of the sun. So, if you're looking for a low-maintenance plant that will brighten up your garden, sunflowers are a great choice. Just don't forget to give them a little drink if the weather is particularly hot or dry.

Best time to visit a sunflower Farm

If you want to see sunflowers in all their glory, the best time to visit a sunflower farm is during the summer months. That's when the flowers are in full bloom, and they provide a stunning backdrop for photos. Of course, you'll also find plenty of bees and other insects buzzing around the flowers during this time of year. So if you're allergic to pollen, you may want to visit a sunflower farm later in the season. The fall months are a great time to see sunflowers, as the leaves begin to change color and the flowers start to droop. But no matter when you visit a sunflower farm, you're sure to be impressed by these beautiful plants.

Profitable sunflower farming

Sunflower farming is a great way to make money. The sunflower is a beautiful flower that can be used for decoration, cooking, and even oil. The best part about sunflower farming is that it is relatively easy to do and does not require a lot of expensive equipment. Sunflowers require special seeds, feeders, and irrigation systems. With a little planning and preparation, sunflower farming can be a profitable business venture.

Here are the steps you need to take to set up a profitable sunflower farming business:

1. Choose the right location: Sunflowers need full sunlight to grow, so make sure you choose a spot that gets at least six hours of sunlight per day.

2. Prepare the soil: Sunflowers need well-drained, fertile soil to thrive. If your soil is not up to par, consider amending it with organic matter such as compost or manure.

3. Choose the right variety: There are many different types of sunflowers, so do your research to choose the best variety for your climate and growing conditions.

4. Start from seed: While you can buy sunflower plants from a nursery, it is much cheaper to start from seed. Sow the seeds in late spring, after the last frost date for your area.

5. Water regularly: Sunflowers are drought-tolerant, but they will produce more flowers if they are kept evenly moist. Water the plants deeply about once a week, or more often if it is very hot and dry.

6. Fertilize monthly: Sunflowers are heavy feeders and will benefit from regular fertilization. Use an all-purpose fertilizer and apply it according to the package directions.

7. Deadhead spent blooms: To encourage continuous flowering, deadhead spent blooms as they begin to fade. Simply cut off the stem below the bloom, being careful not to damage the developing flower buds below.

8. Harvest in fall: Most sunflower varieties will be ready for harvest in mid-to-late summer or early fall when the petals begin to turn brown and drop off naturally. Cut the stems about 6 inches below the flower head and use them fresh or dry them for later use.

With these tips, you can easily set up a profitable sunflower farming business.

You can sell your sunflowers to wholesale markets, florists, and online retailers they are all potential customers. If you're selling directly to consumers, you'll need words like "farm fresh" and "locally grown." People are willing to pay more for sunflowers that are fresh and local, so it's important to emphasize these points. You'll also need to price your sunflowers competitively. Check out the prices at your local grocery store or farmers' market and make sure you're in the same ballpark. And finally, don't forget the power of social media. A strong online presence will help you reach more customers and sell more sunflowers.

So there you have it: with a little hard work and some marketing savvy, you can turn sunflower farming into a profitable business venture.

CHAPTER 8

Cut Flower Farm Layout

There's more to a cut flower farm layout than just sticking a bunch of flowers in the ground and hoping for the best. In order to maximize yield and product quality, farmers must carefully consider the placement of each individual plant. For example, taller varieties should be planted on the north side of the field so that they don't block sunlight from shorter plants. Plants that require a lot of water should be placed near a water source, and those that are susceptible to pests should be kept away from areas where pests are known to congregate. By taking the time to develop a well-designed layout, farmers can ensure that their crops will thrive and produce beautiful blooms all season long.

Space needed for a cut flower garden

When it comes to planning a cut flower garden, the question of space is often one of the first to come up. How much room do you need to grow a healthy crop of flowers? The answer, unfortunately, is not as simple as a number. The amount of space you'll need for your garden will depend on several factors, including the type of flowers you're growing, the climate in your area, and the amount of sun and water your plants will need. However, there are a few general guidelines you can follow to help you plan your garden.

First, most cut flowers will need at least six hours of sunlight per day. If you're limited on space, choose varieties that are known to be compact growers.

Second, aim for at least two square feet of space per plant. This will give your plants enough room to spread their roots and develop into healthy adults.

Don't forget to leave some extra space for paths and walkways. After all, you'll need to be able to reach your flowers to cut them! By following these simple tips, you can ensure that your cut flower garden is both beautiful and practical.

Arranging cut flowers in a garden

As any seasoned gardener knows, arranging cut flowers in a garden is an art form. There are many factors to consider, from the type of flowers you're using to the shape of your vase. But with a little creativity, you can create a beautiful arrangement that will bring life to any garden.

One important factor to consider is the type of flowers you're using. If you're using tall flowers, such as lilies or roses, be sure to place them in the back of the arrangement. This will help support the shorter flowers in front and create a more balanced look. You'll also want to consider the color of your flowers. Try to use a mix of colors for a more vibrant arrangement. And don't be afraid to experiment with different blooms - adding some greenery or filler can really make an arrangement pop.

Pay attention to the shape of your vase. The shape of the vase can really affect the overall look of an arrangement. For example, a tall, slender vase is perfect for a more elegant look, while a wide, shallow vase is ideal for a more casual arrangement. By considering all of these factors, you can create an arrangement that is truly unique and beautiful.

Setting up a garden cutting

A garden cutting is a great way to add interest and variety to your garden. To get started, you will need to choose a location that receives at least six hours of direct sunlight per day. Once you have selected a spot, clear away any debris or plants that might interfere with your design. Next, mark out the area of your garden by cutting with string or stakes. Then, using a spade or trowel, dig a trench around the perimeter of your cutting. The trench should be about six inches deep and six inches wide. Once you have finished digging the trench, remove any remaining debris from the area. Finally, top the soil with two to three inches of compost or organic matter. This will help to improve drainage and prevent weeds from taking root. With a little care and attention, your garden cutting will soon be blooming with beautiful flowers.

Growing cut flowers in winter

Growing cut flowers in winter can be challenging, but it is possible with the right care and attention. One key consideration is the type of flower you choose to grow. Hardier varieties such as roses and carnations are more likely to survive the colder weather, whereas delicate blooms such as lilies and orchids will need to be grown indoors. Another important factor is temperature; both the air and the soil should be kept relatively warm, around 50-60 degrees Fahrenheit. The final consideration is light; during the winter months, days are shorter and sunlight is less intense. As a result, you may need to provide supplemental light in order to encourage your flowers to bloom. With careful planning and attention to detail, it is possible to enjoy a beautiful bouquet of winter flowers.

CONCLUSION

Now that you have all the information you need to get started on your Flower Farm, it is time to put your plan into action. Don't get discouraged if things don't go perfectly at first - it takes time and practice to master the art of flower farming. But with a little hard work and dedication, you can turn your passion for flowers into a thriving business.

Thanks for reading, and I wish you all the best in your floral ventures!